THE HORSE LIBRARY

THE HORSE LIBRARY

DRESSAGE

Betty Bolté

Chelsea House Publishers
Philadelphia

Frontis: JoAnne Gelarden rides Montana Native in the
dressage competition at the Rolex Kentucky Three-Day Event.

CHELSEA HOUSE PUBLISHERS

EDITOR IN CHIEF Sally Cheney
ASSOCIATE EDITOR IN CHIEF Kim Shinners
PRODUCTION MANAGER Pamela Loos
ART DIRECTOR Sara Davis

STAFF FOR DRESSAGE

EDITOR Sally Cheney
ASSOCIATE ART DIRECTOR Takeshi Takahashi
SERIES DESIGNER Keith Trego

CHESTNUT PRODUCTIONS AND CHOPTANK SYNDICATE, INC.

EDITORIAL AND PICTURE RESEARCH Mary Hull and Norman Macht
LAYOUT AND PRODUCTION Lisa Hochstein

http://www.chelseahouse.com

First Printing

1 3 5 7 9 8 6 4 2

Library of Congress Cataloguing-in-Publication Data Applied For.

Horse Library SET: 0-7910-6650-9
Dressage: 0-7910-6656-8

TABLE OF CONTENTS

Sir Duba, one of the traveling Lipizzan stallions who perform all over the world, practices his capriole before a performance. The brand on his left flank serves as identification.

THE HISTORY
OF DRESSAGE

You might think that dressage is a new way of teaching a horse. Actually, the noted Greek historian and general, Xenophon, created the art of dressage in Greece in 400 B.C. According to Xenophon, "If the rider is not in harmony with the nature of the animal, then it will perform as a burden with no display of pleasure." Dressage training increases the horse's ability and desire to perform for the rider. Because dressage is excellent training for any equestrian discipline, it has grown in popularity. The classical form of dressage we use today was developed in the royal courts of Europe in the 17th and 18th centuries.

Dressage is French for "training" and it is a way to teach the horse and rider to communicate and cooperate. The United States Dressage Federation (USDF) says "requiring the power and precision of gymnastics, and the grace and subtlety of ballet, dressage challenges mental preparation as well as physical prowess."

Today more than ever the emphasis in horse training is shifting to the discipline of dressage. This is because dressage makes sure the horse and rider are working together to accomplish a harmony. Dressage is an art in which the horse and rider become "two hearts with one mind."

Dressage works to improve the horse's build and suppleness. It also improves the natural gaits of walk, trot and

 Dressage Is For Everybody

Lucy Walker won a U.S. Dressage Federation bronze medal on her horse Jazzy. But that didn't stop her from taking Jazzy on a cattle drive. One Saturday, Walker visited Bob Velasquez's 5000-acre ranch in Ojai, California, ready to see how Jazzy would take to the cattle. After receiving her instructions for the day, she was assigned to ride with roundup boss Bob Yanez, a horseman with 65 years of experience.

Jazzy was touchy and anxious at first, but soon the rough going settled him down and he learned how to stand his ground against the cattle, even herding cattle back onto the trail. Walker was pleased to answer the other riders' questions about Jazzy's fitness and quiet manner, and explained how dressage works to make a horse's conditioning better by working all the muscles correctly. Walker and Jazzy proved that dressage is a great foundation training for whatever you want your horse to learn— from eventing to rounding up cattle.

canter. Improving the gaits makes riding the horse more fun. When a horse is trained properly, it allows the horse to be supple on both sides, to want to respond and do what is asked of him. The horse will move forward easily and with lots of energy to its stride.

Not only does dressage improve the horse's abilities, it also works to better the rider's seat, coordination, and feel of the horse. Through subtle weight shifts, leg pressure, and signals along the reins, the rider talks to the horse. The rider must remain in an upright posture with "independent" legs and hands (hands able to move separately from each other and from the legs) in order to be in harmony with the horse. These skills take many hours of proper training and practice to achieve and provide an on-going challenge to the rider. Once the skills are acquired, the rider has the immense satisfaction of riding in personal harmony with the horse, making the time in the saddle a true pleasure.

One of the greatest examples of the feats that horse and rider can accomplish through dressage is found in the famous Lipizzaner stallions of the Spanish Riding School of Vienna. The Lipizzaners perform haute école (high school) moves known as the "airs above the ground." These moves include the courbette, levade, and capriole. In the courbette, the horse stands on its hind legs, then jumps with both hind legs together, and the forelegs off the ground. The levade consists of the horse standing on its rear legs, with its haunches at a 45-degree angle. The capriole is performed when a stallion leaps into the air, pulls its forelegs under its chest, and kicks out sharply behind at the height of the leap. Each of these moves was originally designed to make military horses valuable combat assets. By pulling back suddenly in the air, the horse could prevent its rider from being attacked with a sword, and by leaping and kicking he could present a threatening image to foot soldiers. Today these moves are seen only during Lipizzaner performances.

The Lipizzan lives thirty to thirty-five years, a long time for a horse. They normally are born black and gradually change to white over six to ten years. Sometimes a colt is born white, but very seldom. When a colt is born white, it receives special treatment and duties throughout its life. The Lipizzan stands 14.2 to 15.2 hands at maturity.

Breeders believe horses from Carthage provided the basis for the Lipizzaner more than 2000 years ago. The Carthaginian horses were bred to a Vilano, a Pyrenees horse, along with Arabian and Barbary horses to create the beautiful Andalusian horses of ancient Spain.

After Spain defeated the Moors, it started exporting Andalusian horses to other countries. Two important stud farms were created in Italy and Denmark. The Italian blood-line, known as the Neapolitan, was famous in Europe, while the Danish breeding also produced excellent horses.

Around 1562, Archduke Maximilian, who later became Emperor of Austria, bred Spanish horses. Then in 1580, Archduke Karl created a royal stud farm among the hills of Karst, near Trieste, in the town of Lipizza. The rough terrain, with its rocks and hills, produced little for the horses to eat. Fortunately, the horses did well despite the lack of good grazing. They grew stronger and faster and were able to run longer distances.

These tough little horses were owned primarily by the nobility and the military aristocracy. The stallions became fighting horses, trained to perform leaps and to kick out behind them so they could be used in battles against foot soldiers. The trained Lipizzaner stallions were very intimidating. The smart white mares were used as coach horses.

An engraving of a French cavalry school shows the high-school dressage moves known as the "airs above the ground," which were performed before European royalty in the 17th and 18th centuries.

In 1781, during the Napoleonic Wars, 300 horses were evacuated from Lipizza and taken on a 40-day march to Stuhlweissenburg in order to save them from the fighting. Once the war was over, the horses were brought back to Lipizza. Then in 1805 they were moved to Slavonia, and in 1806 taken to Karad in Hungary. When they were once again returned to Lipizza, they had to leave almost immediately to flee the armies of France.

The Lipizzaners lived along the Pisza River from 1809 to 1815, but the land there weakened the breed. Only by breeding to horses outside of the Lipizzaner herd over a period of years were the Lipizzaners restored to their previous condition and standards.

One hundred years later, in May 1915, the Lipizzans were divided into two groups. One group went to Laxenburg outside Vienna, the other to Kladrub. In 1918 Lipizza became part of Italy. The two governments, Italian and Austrian, divided the Lipizzaner herd.

A Lipizzan stallion from the Spanish Riding School of Vienna performs a courbette, a move requiring tremendous concentration and balance. First the horse balances on his hindquarters with his forelegs lifted, then he jumps forward.

During World War II, in early 1945, allied forces advanced toward Vienna, home of the famous Spanish Riding School. The head of the School, Colonel Alois Podhajsky, had the horses moved by train to Upper Austria,

200 miles from Vienna, to a small town called St. Martin's. The horses were kept on the estate of a friend of Podhajsky. When the U.S. Third Army arrived, one officer recognized Podhajsky and sent word to General George S. Patton. Podhajsky and Patton were friends, and had competed in equestrian events at the Olympic Games in years past.

Podhajsky wanted to ensure the safety of the Lipizzaners and arranged a demonstration for Patton and Undersecretary of War Robert Patterson. Patton's training as a cavalryman at the U.S. Military Academy at West Point, New York, enabled him to appreciate the value of the white stallions. The men were so impressed by the performance that Patton agreed to take the horses under the U.S. Army's protection until they could return to Vienna. On April 26, 1945, a captured German general revealed that Lipizzan mares and foals were being held at the German Remount Depot in Hostau, along with Allied prisoners of war who were caring for the horses.

Patton freed the horses and prisoners before approaching Russian troops arrived. The German officers helped the Americans rescue the horses and prisoners, as they feared the Russians would destroy the horses and thus the breed. The Americans saved 150 Lipizzans: stallions, mares, and two- and three-year-old colts.

When the war ended, the Russians and the Czechs started arguing over who owned the horses. The horses were moved into Germany until Colonel Podhajsky received them at Linz. The story of the daring rescue of the Lipizzaners was later made into a Disney movie, *The Miracle of the White Horses*. Today each registered Lipizzan is branded with its bloodline. There are six recognized bloodlines, tracing back to these stallions: The Dane, "Pluto," 1765; The Neapolitans, "Conversano," 1767; "Maestosa," 1773;

"Favory," 1799; "Neapolitano," 1790; and the Arab, "Siglavy," from the stables of Prince Schwarzenberg, 1810.

In the United States, there has also been a long relationship between dressage and the military. For almost 150 years, the U.S. Military Academy at West Point, New York, included basic horsemanship and riding as part of a cadet's daily schoolwork. Until the 1950s, riding was a daily part of the cadet's life. Those cadets who chose to could attend the cavalry school at Fort Riley, Kansas, where cavalry officers spent a year studying horsemanship, equitation, and horse management, as well as weapons and military tactics. Each officer was required to know how to shoe his own horse, to know equine anatomy, disease, lameness, and treatment, and to ride very well.

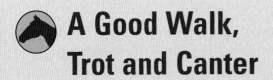

A Good Walk, Trot and Canter

When a horse performs a "good walk," each stride covers a good distance. He will overtrack (his hind feet step over his front hoof prints), and he moves freely from the shoulder, walking in a defined four-beat rhythm.

A good trot consists of a defined two-beat rhythm, with lots of impulsion from his hind legs so that his hind legs step under his body and into the hoof prints of the forefeet. The horse also maintains a steady rhythm that does not change with the speed of the trot.

A horse performs a good canter when he is well balanced, maintaining a defined three-beat rhythm that makes him collected underneath the rider.

Lipizzaner broodmares turned out to pasture at a breeding farm in Lipica, Slovenia. Lipizzaners are dark-colored when they are born, but they get increasingly lighter with age. By age three they have begun to gray, and by the time they are ten they are pure white.

Fifty-five officers attended the cavalry school each year. Of those, about ten would advance to a second year to attend the advanced course in equitation. This course was known as the premier American horsemanship program. The life of a cavalryman revolved around horses, to the point that not only did they ride eight to twelve hours each day, but their wives and children also rode. In 1912, when the Olympic Committee decided to include equestrian competition at the Olympics, the rules allowed only military officers and military-owned or associated mounts to compete.

In January 1912, the United States War Department sent out Special Order No. 20 stating that the cavalry should select and prepare a team for competition at the first Olympic equestrian competition. The training for the event was held at Fort Riley with Captain Guy V. Henry Jr. heading the program. They trained eighteen horses for the Games. However, the government provided no funding for the team to train and travel to the Olympics. The cavalry gave performances around the country to raise money for the fund. The team won a bronze in the three-day event, and finished fourth in the Prix des Nations, the show jumping competition.

The United States didn't finish in the medals in dressage until the 1932 Games in Los Angeles, California. The U.S. team of Hiram Tuttle on Olympic, Isaac Kitts on American Lady, and Alvin Moor on Water Pat earned the bronze medal in team dressage, and Hiram Tuttle and Olympic won the individual bronze.

The United States Equestrian team (USET) did not win another medal until 1992, when Charlotte Bredahl on Monsieur, Robert Dover on Lectron, and Carol Lavelle on Gifted secured the team bronze medal. The USET went on to win the team bronze again in 1996 with Michelle Gibson on Peron, Robert Dover on Metallic, Steffen Peters on Udon, and Guenter Seidel on Graf George. In 2000 the USET dressage team captured the bronze team medal once again with Sue Blinks on Flim Flam, Robert Dover on Ranier, Guenter Seidel on Foltaire, and Christine Traurig on Etienne.

Perhaps the most successful national equestrian team is Germany's, which has finished in the medals in both team and individual dressage competition at most of the Olympic Games since 1912. In team competition, Germany has collected ten gold medals, two silver medals, and one bronze. In individual competition, the Germans have earned seven gold medals, six silver medals, and seven bronze medals. At the 2000 Olympics in Sydney, they took the gold medal in team dressage for the fifth Games in a row, and silver and bronze medals in the individual competition. Sweden has consistently placed in the medals as well, along with Switzerland, Russia (the former U.S.S.R.), and the Netherlands.

2

Anky van Grunsven of
the Netherlands, shown
performing a levade with
Bonfire at the 2000 Olympics,
has won the Dressage World
Cup five times.

PREPARING TO LEARN DRESSAGE

Except for a deep-seated saddle, dressage does not require much equipment. Most people use an English saddle of some type, but you can use a Western saddle if you are more comfortable riding in one. The seat should help you sit in the middle and deepest part of the saddle to keep you well balanced.

You will also need a simple bridle with a snaffle bit. A snaffle bit allows only direct pressure on your horse or pony's mouth, so that when you pull on the reins there aren't any other actions applied to his mouth. The harsher bits force your pony to comply. Dressage is about harmony between horse and rider, a willingness on the part of the horse to do what you ask him to do. If you reach the higher levels of dressage, you might use a double bridle with four reins and two bits—a snaffle bit and a curb bit.

Eventually you might want to purchase a dressage whip, which is longer than a typical riding crop. The longer whip allows you to flick your pony's side without removing your hands from the reins. Some advanced riders, and some of the Lipizzaner riders, use two whips—one on either side—to communicate with the horse.

Western saddles are not allowed in recognized dressage competitions. Upper levels of dressage require a dressage saddle with a deep seat, specifically designed for correct leg placement along your horse's sides. These saddles are tailored to fit you and your horse, and therefore can be very expensive.

The first thing you'll need to do is locate a good trainer. Anyone can say they know how to teach you how to ride. Most states do not require a special license or certification for a riding teacher. In order to learn dressage correctly, you need a trainer who was taught correctly and who can teach you. Someone may be an award-winning rider, but that doesn't mean that person can tell you how to ride.

Word of mouth is the best way to locate a good trainer. If you are currently taking riding lessons, ask your instructor. Ask at tack shops. Go to shows and see who rides well, then find out who trains them. The importance of a good trainer cannot be overemphasized.

Your trainer will teach you how to communicate to your horse using aids, how to ride the basic dressage figures, how to supple yourself and your horse, and how to achieve free forward movement, obedience, and straightness from your horse.

When riding a dressage circle or curve, the horse's head should bend in the direction of the circle, as shown by Etienne, a 12-year-old Westphalian gelding ridden by Christine Traurig of the United States.

The basic items you will need to take a dressage lesson include a riding, or schooling helmet that has been approved by the American Society for Testing Materials (ASTM) and the Safety Equipment Institute (SEI). You will need hard-soled boots that have a low heel. You never want to ride in sneakers or softsoled shoes as they do not slide out of the stirrup as easily, creating a safety hazard should you need to dismount in a hurry. They also allow your foot to bend and flex and will make your foot hurt if you ride for very long.

While many people have ridden in blue jeans, they are not the most comfortable pants to wear. Nor do they allow your leg to fit as snugly to the horse as is required in dressage. You might want to invest in a pair of jodhpurs—stretchy pants that fit over jodhpur or paddock boots. Jodphurs no longer need to flare out at the thigh to fit well; now they hug your legs. Jodhpurs have an elastic strap that slips under your boot, in front of the heel. You can also find riding jeans that have a knee patch sewn into the stretchy jeans fabric.

Whatever you choose to wear, be sure your trainer can see your waist clearly—no bulky sweaters or heavy jackets that hide your waist. Your trainer needs to see your position in the saddle.

 Types of Whips

There are many kinds of whips you can use to correct your horse. Most people know of the crop, which is about two-and-a-half feet long with a one-inch loop at the end. The loop makes a stinging pop on the horse and encourages him forward. The bat is shorter than a crop, with a wider loop that makes a louder slapping sound. In order to prevent pulling on your pony's mouth, you should always put both reins in one hand before hitting your pony with a crop or bat. The dressage whip is about three feet long, with a lash on the end that flicks the pony's side. You do not have to remove your hand from the rein to use a dressage whip.

Your trainer will help you learn the basics so that you are riding as safely as possible. Just like you had to learn the letters of the alphabet before you could write a story, horses need to learn how to respond to the signals of the rider before performing any work for the rider.

Natural aids –the rider's legs, hands, voice, and seat—are used most in dressage. The rider's legs guide the horse by applying pressure against the horse's side to "push" the horse away from the leg. So, to tell the horse to turn to the left, the rider presses the right leg against the horse's side and "pushes" the horse to the left. Much of steering your pony is done with your legs, not your hands.

Your hands are used to help guide and balance the horse. You will start out with larger moves with your hands, but as you and your pony learn, your hand movements will decrease. At times, it is necessary to keep the horse's attention by working the reins just a little. This helps keep him focused on his work.

You may use your voice in many situations, such as during practices, trail riding, or running a cross-country course. If you've ever been to a horse show, you might have heard the rider comment to the horse, usually in praise. However, in dressage competition you won't hear the rider talk to the horse because even clucking to your horse is penalized in the dressage ring. No verbal communication is allowed in dressage competition.

The way you sit on the saddle also tells the horse what you expect. A slight shift of your seat bones and your weight tells the horse to move in a certain direction, or slow down, or many other commands. Your head is very heavy, and how you carry your head also tells the pony where you want to go. You should always keep your head level, eyes looking where you want your pony to go.

Ridden by USET member Christine Traurig, Etienne shows off his dressage training: his head is rounded and flexed at the poll, and his trot is well-balanced.

The artificial riding aids—items such as spurs, whips, and crops—back up the natural aids to correct the horse. There are many types of spurs, and many types of whips and crops, each designed to help in a specific way. By combining the natural and artificial aids, the rider tells the horse which direction to go, and what he is expected to do. Through many hours of repetition and practice, you and your horse will develop a trust that will carry you through any exercise.

As you progress in dressage, your trainer will teach you how to guide your horse through several basic figures: a circle, a half-circle, and a diagonal. They may seem easy because they are simple geometric shapes, but there is a right way to ride a figure and a wrong way.

The typical size circle in dressage is 20 meters across. This is the same size as the short width of the dressage arena. The 20-meter circle is used in many training situations, and is also a good size for lunging your horse. Lunging is a technique used for conditioning a horse with or without a rider. The horse works on its gaits—walk, trot, and canter—as it circles a person holding a long, flat lead line called a lunge line, which is attached to the horse's bridle. Side reins are often used to ensure that the horse's head is carried correctly, that is, that the horse is rounded, or "on the bit," as he moves.

The circle is ridden so that your horse "bends" around the circle. This means that the horse is looking around the circle without having his head too far toward the center and with his feet on the circle. The rider presses his outside leg (the one away from the center of the circle) against the horse slightly behind the girth, while the inside leg is pressed at the girth. By having your legs in this position, your outside leg is pushing the horse around your inside leg. The reins are kept as still as possible, with a slight tension on the inside rein. Depending on your horse, you may have to make some other slight adjustments to teach him to "bend" properly. If the horse's head angles away from the circle, he is said to be "bending in the wrong direction." This may be because of too much tension on the outside rein.

The diagonal is a straight line that cuts from one corner of the arena to the opposite one at the far end. The horse should travel in a straight line, not in a zig-zag line or bowed line. Again, this sounds easy, but it takes quite a bit of practice to accomplish.

The half-circle is used to change direction, or "change rein." Starting along the rail of the arena, you begin to make a circle, then halfway around you turn and ride a diagonal back to the rail.

Suppling exercises are used to stretch your muscles and get them ready to work. They also improve your balance and add to your confidence. The United States Pony Club (USPC) describes several exercises for the beginning rider in their *Manual of Horsemanship.* You might want to try foot circles, ankle stretches, leg swings, poll and croup touches, and the "around the world."

To begin, have someone hold your pony at a halt. Drop your stirrups. Foot circles are done exactly as they sound: you rotate your foot so that it makes a circle in the air, without moving your legs. Ankle stretches are merely pointing your toe up and then down, again while keeping your leg still. To do leg swings, swing one leg forward (from the knee down) and the other backward, while letting your toes hang down. Poll and croup touches are stretches you do, with your feet in the stirrups, where you reach for the space between your horse's ears, and then reach for the top of his tail.

Most kids like to do the "around the world" once they've done it a few times. Have someone hold your pony, and then cross over your stirrups to get them out of your way. Check your balance, then swing your right leg over the horse's neck until you're sitting sideways. Swing your left leg over your horse's rump until you're facing backward. Continue around until you're facing forward again. Once you've mastered that, try it without using your hands.

Colonel Ljungquist: Dressage Promoter

One man, Colonel Bengt Ljungquist, an officer in the Swedish cavalry, helped revive and promote the art and sport of dressage in the United States. Ljungquist was an outstanding athlete. He had already competed in four Olympics and won two medals in fencing competition. It wasn't until 1964 at the Olympics in Tokyo that he competed for the first time in equestrian events.

Upon his retirement, Ljungquist emigrated to America in 1970 and took up residence in Maryland. He became the resident trainer at Idlewilde Farm in Davidsonville. There he worked with Linda Zang, a U.S. dressage rider and trainer who later became an Olympic dressage judge. Riders came from across the country to learn from him. Ljungquist's methods were so popular that the U.S. Equestrian Team invited him to coach the 1974 World Championship dressage squad. In 1975, he helped the U.S. Pan American Games team win a gold medal.

The high point of his career was helping the U.S. dressage team win a bronze medal at the 1976 Olympics in Montreal. The team consisted of Hilda Gurney on Keen, Dorothy Morkis on Monaco, and Edith Master on Dahlwitz.

In 1976 Ljungquist wrote a book called the *Practical Dressage Manual*, in which he defined his methods and philosophies. He also wrote an essay titled "The American Dressage Outlook" for an anthology called *The U.S. Equestrian Team Book of Riding*. In part he said, "I believe that finding and using good instructors is essential to the future of the sport."

Ljungquist coached the U.S. dressage team for a few more years, then chose to focus on private instruction at Idlewilde and at Virginia's Morven Park International Equestrian Institute. In 1979, at age 69, he died of a heart attack while visiting in Sweden.

Just as you need to stretch your muscles and be fit, so does your horse. The USPC defines suppleness as the horse's "ability to shift his balance forward and backward quickly and smoothly, and to turn easily." When your pony is supple, he will be easier to ride because he's more bendable and easy to turn.

When your pony is stiff, it means he does not turn easily and is not as much fun to ride. He might even move forward in an awkward, crooked way. Stiffness can be due to poor training or riding or a problem with the horse's soundness. Young, green horses are often stiff just because they haven't been trained properly.

Each horse is more supple on one side than the other. Through proper training, you can help your pony become more balanced and less stiff on his weaker side. Without proper training, a pony might become one-sided—that is, better at going in one direction than the other. He might also be difficult for you to turn and not be able to pick up the correct lead when cantering.

Specific exercises will help you keep your pony supple. You should work on transitions from one gait to another (walk to trot, trot to walk, trot to canter, etc.) and ride them so that you use your legs and seat first, then your hands, to tell your pony to change gaits.

A horse's hindquarters are what push him forward. Your horse should always be working primarily from behind to propel himself forward. His hind legs should be under him, and he should be stepping into your hand. His neck shouldn't show signs of tension, and neither should his back. He should also not resist your rein contact.

Your horse should do what you ask when you ask. When he does, he is being obedient and this is called being "in front of the rider's leg." If he does not respond immediately, you might need to correct him by tapping him with your crop or whip. Merely applying a stronger leg pressure might make him less responsive in the future. Your trainer can help you decide how best to respond to disobedience.

Some dressage judges view the horse's tail as a signal of whether the horse is being willing and obedient. If the tail is hanging comfortably, or swishing lightly from side to side, he's relaxed and obedient. If the horse is flicking the tail up and down, or harshly from side to side, he is resisting the rider's commands.

Your supple horse can now learn to be straight and carry his head and his hindquarters in one line. Having your pony straight makes sure his spine is aligned correctly. He will step with his back feet along the tracks of his front feet, and if he is reaching well, he'll even overstep his front hoof prints. When riding on a circle or a curve, your pony will bend so that he's looking along the circle that he's moving on. His head will turn slightly so that you can just see his eyelashes on the side closest to the center of the circle (the inside).

The USPC teaches dressage as a sound, safe basis for a rider to progress to jumping. While dressage is a recognized sport by itself, the USPC encourages all its members to participate in dressage, cross-country, and show jumping. A prime mission of the USPC is to provide quality instruction at reduced costs. Mounted meetings are usually held once or twice a month. You must have access to a pony or horse, but you do not need to own one to join. Anyone under 21 years old may participate. Each member is rated using letters and numbers. A new rider starts out as "unrated." Once the member can perform basic riding skills and knows a little bit about their tack and pony, they can become a D1. The ratings progress through D2, D3, C1,

A horse's "lead" is the front leg that he first moves forward on; dressage teaches the horse to change leads readily and to even change leads mid-stride.

C2, C3, B, H/A, and A. Those members that achieve the rating of A are fully qualified to operate a stable, train horses, teach lessons, and compete at the highest levels of competition.

The U.S. Dressage Federation (USDF) consists of more than 34,000 members and more than 120 local dressage clubs across the country. The USDF conducts a year-end award program for competitors across the country who have scored well on their dressage tests. The USDF also provides training for judges, instructors, and trainers, and it conducts special programs for young riders and adult amateurs.

Germany's Ulla Salzberger and Rusty, a Hanoverian gelding, show off their dressage training while competing at the 2000 Olympics. Hanoverians, or Westphalians, are one of the most popular breeds for dressage competition.

DRESSAGE HORSES

Any horse or pony is capable of learning the basics of dressage. However, there are several breeds that possess the personality and temperament to win awards in dressage on a consistent basis. These breeds, which are favored by Olympic dressage riders, include: the Trakehner, Hanoverian, Holsteiner, Oldenburg, and Swedish Warmblood. Each of these horses was bred to be an excellent saddle horse with great strength and a willing, kind temperament.

The Trakehner is also known as an East Prussian horse. The Trakehner is descended from a cross between the Smudish horses of Lithuania mixed with Arab and Thoroughbred blood.

Smudish horses range in height from 13 to 15 hands, and are an ancient breed from the Baltic States. William I of Prussia started the Trakehnen Stud in East Prussia in 1732. He used the best Arabian stallions from Poland and some from his Royal Stud in Wurtemburg to begin the breed. The Trakehner was well suited to be a cavalry horse and was also used for light farm work because of its endurance. Through the introduction of Thoroughbred blood, the Trakehner grew in height and improved in conformation. These changes helped broaden the range of uses for the Trakehner. This lively horse stands 16 to 16.2 hands and can be any solid color. The Trakehner is known for its kindness and stamina.

One of the most popular of the German breeds, the Hanoverian is descended from the war-horses that carried armor-wearing knights into battle during the Middle Ages. It was once used as a cavalry mount. Today's Hanoverian exhibits smoother lines and finer muscling thanks to an

 A Winning Team of Horses

The horses ridden by the U.S. at the 2000 Sydney Olympics Team Dressage Competition were a mix of breeds.
- Etienne, a 12-year-old Westphalian gelding, ridden by Christine Traurig
- Foltaire, a 13-year-old Dutch Warmblood, ridden by Guenter Seidel
- Flim Flam, a 13-year-old Hanoverian gelding, ridden by Sue Blinks
- Ranier, a 9-year-old Oldenburg gelding, ridden by Robert Dover

USET member Robert Dover rides Ranier, a 9-year-old Oldenburg gelding, in Olympic dressage competition at the 2000 Olympics.

introduction of English Thoroughbred blood from 1714 through 1837, which lightened the horse. These English Thoroughbreds were closely related to the foundation Arabian sires: the Darley Arabian, the Byerley Turk, and the Godolphin Barb. The organization responsible for overseeing the registry of Hanoverians is the State Stud at Celle, Germany, which was founded in 1735. Since the 1940s, breeders have worked towards creating a fine competition horse. They added more Thoroughbred blood to the line, which has improved the breed so that today it is in demand as a dressage horse and a jumper. The Hanoverian stands 16 to 17 hands and is usually bay, black, brown, or chestnut. The Hanoverian is also known in some regions as a Westphalian.

The Holsteiner has heavy horses in its ancestry, but by breeding the Holsteiner with Yorkshire Coach Horses and English Thoroughbreds during the 19th century, breeders made the Holsteiner suitable for light harness and saddle work. After World War II, more Thoroughbred blood was added to the breed, making it an all-round saddle horse with a great ability for show jumping. The Holsteiner has strong front and hindquarters, coupled with a deep girth and short legs with strong bones. This mild-tempered horse is usually black, brown, or bay, and stands 15.3 to 16.2 hands high.

The Oldenburg is the heaviest warmblood from Germany. Its ancestry dates back to 17th century, when it was bred with Friesians, which were known as good carriage horses. In addition, the Oldenburg also has Spanish, Neapolitan, Barb, Thoroughbred, Cleveland Bay, Norman, and Hanoverian blood. As the need for carriage horses dwindled during the early part of the 20th century, more Thoroughbred and Norman blood was added, producing an all-around saddle horse. The Oldenburg stands 16.2 to 17.2 hands, with rather short, strong legs, and it is favored for its strong back and deep girth.

For the past three hundred years, breeders have selectively bred the Swedish Warmblood as a fine saddle horse. In fact, the breed was initially used as a cavalry horse. At first, crosses between Spanish, Friesian, and Oriental bloodlines were used, with some Thoroughbred, Arab,

USET member Guenter Seidel competes with Foltaire, a 13-year-old Dutch Warmblood. Dutch Warmbloods were created by crossing two native Dutch breeds, the Gelderlander and the Groningen, and adding Thoroughbred blood.

Hanoverian, and Trakehner blood more recently added to the breed. The result is a strong, good-tempered saddle horse with a wonderful ability in dressage and driving events. The Swedish Warmblood is a heavy horse standing 16.2 hands on average. Swedish Warmbloods may be any solid color.

While these are the top breeds known for dressage, they are not the only ones that can perform well. Thoroughbreds,

American Warmbloods, and Dutch Warmbloods are just a few of the other breeds that excel in dressage. Generally, a horse with a long back has a harder time becoming round. When looking for a horse, you want to look for one with a shorter back. You also need the horse to have impulsion when it moves—a lightness to its gait and a willingness to move forward at your command.

German and Swedish breeds tend to be the most successful in dressage and thus the most popular. They have both been modified by Thoroughbred blood. Breeding in Germany is carefully controlled and is strongly emphasized. For example, when talking about horses in Germany, the conversation centers on the pedigree of the horse. German horse breeders have focused on breeding horses for temperament rather than solely for speed, as Thoroughbreds have been bred. Thus, the Hanoverian, Trakehner, and Holstein studs all continue to produce top quality, kind-mannered horses.

American breeders, however, are also working to produce top dressage horses. In 1999, four American-bred horses finished in the Horse of the Year standings. A five-year-old Swedish Warmblood, On Air, owned by Dana Clark of Loganville, Georgia, was named the American Horse Shows Association and American Banker's Insurance Company Open Division Regional Champion. Lilac, an eight-year-old Trakehner mare owned by Whit Watkins, was named the United States Dressage Federation (USDF) Third Level Horse of the Year for Freestyle, as well as the Federation Equestre Internationale (FEI) Champion at a New Mexico Dressage show. Then there's Windwalzer, a 14-year-old Trakehner stallion, owned by Flora Jean Weiss. Windwalzer was named the 2000 California Dressage Society (CDS) Horse of the Year, as well as champion of the CDS Grand

Prix Freestyle. G Tudor, a 12-year-old Dutch Warmblood owned by Cherri Reiber, won the 2000 Dressage at the Devon Grand Prix Freestyle Qualifier and the Grand Prix Freestyle. G Tudor also won the World Cup U.S. League Final in 2000. So while Europe has a leg up on America, judges and breeders agree that Americans are making progress in breeding dressage horses.

To perform the piaffe, a horse must raise its legs calmly and rhythmically in an elevated trot while remaining in place.

4

COMPETITIVE DRESSAGE

O nly a small percentage of horses possess the conformation, strength, and temperament needed to win an international dressage competition. However, you can compete at lower levels without needing a perfect dressage horse. The United States Dressage Federation (USDF), United States Combined Training Association (USCTA), and United States Pony Club (USPC) all encourage their members to enjoy competing at their level of training with whatever horse is available to them. In fact, many dressage riders only work to better their personal score. Each test becomes a yardstick of how their training program measures up against the standards.

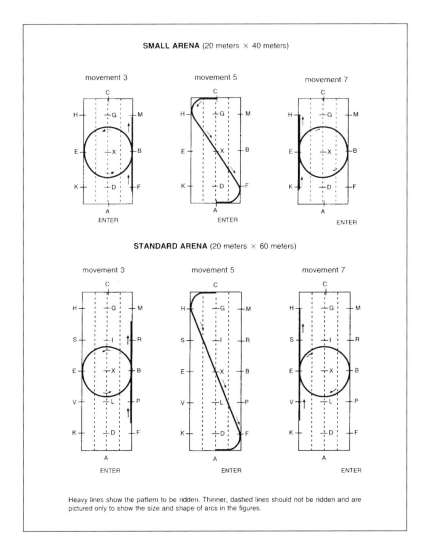

During a dressage test, riders follow a specified course, riding toward the different letters, or points, of the arena, as outlined in the dressage test.

As you begin competing, you'll most likely attend unrecognized schooling shows in your area. This means that the USDF does not track points for ribbons earned at these shows. These shows are relaxed and ideal for beginners, as they provide an opportunity to see how competitions work. You will also learn about show ring etiquette—essential rules of behavior for the show ring.

Prior to entering a competition, you might want to go to several shows and watch how experienced competitors handle entering and exiting the show ring, how they are dressed, and how the horses are turned out for the show. Your first year of showing is one in which you will learn a lot. Keep smiling even on those days when things don't go your way. Everyone is learning how to compete better, even those people who've been competing for years. By attending shows you will learn important things such as where you need to park your trailer to unload, what you need to bring to the show facilities, and how to become more familiar with the routines of showing.

Buy a special journal to keep track of your shows and the results. You might want to include details of the show grounds—what problems you encountered, how long it took to get there, the judges' names, and their comments on your ride. Writing down how you and your horse performed at each show, especially what you need to work on, will help you track the progress of your show season.

Your attire for a show should be as clean and neat as possible. Appearances do count with the judges. Once you're dressed, slip a loose fitting pair of pants and a baggy shirt over your outfit (except the coat) to keep your clothes clean while you prepare your horse for your class. Schooling shows allow you to wear jodhpurs and paddock boots, with a white shirt and riding coat. Unlike a typical sport coat that doesn't always feel comfortable when you are mounted, a riding coat is specially designed to allow for freer movement while riding. If the weather is hot, the judge may waive the need for a coat in the ring. However, you must wear a helmet and boots. Black gloves are recommended to protect your hands and to reduce the potential for a distracting contrast of your hand to your coat sleeve.

Upper level dressage competitions have fancier outfits including tall dress boots, breeches, a white shirt with stock tie and pin, and a riding coat. The international level competitors wear a shadbelly—a special coat with tails. A top hat or bowler replaces the safety helmet for upper level dressage only.

Schooling shows do not require that you braid your horse's mane, however, they provide the perfect opportunity to practice. The best way to learn to braid is to find someone who knows how and is willing to teach you. They can walk your through the following steps.

The first step in braiding is to pull the mane, that is, to remove some of the mane hairs so that the mane is shorter and more even. This way the braids will be the same length. Then, working with a clean mane (you don't want your pony's dandruff showing through the base of the braids), dampen the hair and separate it into even sections about three finger widths wide each. Each of these sections of hair is then braided and secured with braiding rubber bands or heavy braiding thread. The number of sections will vary with your horse's neck length—smaller and tighter braids tend to make a short neck look longer, larger looser and more upright braids to make a long neck look shorter. Having someone show you how to braid is the best plan as there are different styles and methods from which to choose. If necessary, ask at shows or around the barn where you take lessons. Someone will know how to braid. Once you've learned the basics, you can practice until your braids look neat and polished.

All dressage tests are performed in rectangular arenas. Lower level tests are ridden in a small arena that measures

The U.S.A.'s Susan Blinks performs a half-pass with Flim Flam, a 13-year-old Hanoverian gelding. In a half-pass, a horse appears to be crossing its legs as it moves forward.

20 x 40 meters. Upper level tests are ridden in large arenas that measure 20 x 60 meters. Letters placed at specific points around the outside of the arena mark the points

where different elements of the test are to be performed. The letters used in beginning level tests are A, K, E, H, C, M, B, and F. The center of the arena is understood to be marked with an imaginary X. A few additional points are marked for upper level tests: R, S, V, P, L, G, D, and I. The odd mix of letters was determined many years ago, and no one knows exactly why anymore.

There are several levels of dressage for you to work through. The tests build upon each other, so that you are continually adding to the abilities of your horse. As you and your horse progress through the levels, you'll notice that riding becomes more pleasurable even as the challenges continue.

The beginning levels of dressage are the Introductory Level and the Training Level. The Introductory Level test simply requires your horse to be obedient at a brisk walk and trot along the rail and in large circles. The Training Level test requires obedience at a walk, trot, and canter on the rail, in large 20-meter diameter circles, and in serpentines. The tests at the beginning levels take approximately 4 to 6 minutes to perform.

The First Level tests add smaller 15- and 10-meter diameter circles. This level also calls for you to lengthen your horse's stride at the walk and trot. You will need to know how to leg-yield, or have your horse move away from your leg sideways, and to counter canter, which is cantering on the wrong lead.

Second Level tests add changes to gaits, asking for medium and collected gaits. You will also need to know how to shoulder-in and haunches-in. This is when the horse angles his shoulder or his haunches along a straight line. Again you will need to counter canter, but you will also have to demonstrate smooth walk-to-canter transitions. Finally, you'll need to show your horse is able to make a half turn on his haunches while walking.

Third Level tests add a serpentine at the canter, where you ride a "snaking" line between specific points in the arena. Extended gaits demonstrate your horse's controlled speed. Now you not only counter-canter, but you must also perform a flying change of lead, in which your horse changes his leading front leg while cantering. Finally, you'll perform the half-pass at the trot and canter. The half-pass is a move in which the horse faces forward but moves diagonally, appearing to cross his legs as he trots.

Fourth Level dressage tests requires flying changes of lead every four strides and every three strides, canter half-pirouettes, and a trotting zigzag half-pass.

The highest competitive level is the Federation Equestre Internationale (FEI) International Level. At this level, you'll perform flying lead changes every two strides and every one stride, as well as the piaffe, a calm, elevated trot in place, the passage, a slow motion trot, and full canter pirouettes, in which your horse must pivot rhythmically. The first three tests at this level are the Prix St. Georges, Intermediate I, and Intermediate II. The last and highest stage is Grand

Dressage Scores and What They Mean

0	Not performed
1	Very bad
2	Bad
3	Fairly bad
4	Insufficient
5	Sufficient
6	Satisfactory
7	Fairly good
8	Good
9	Very good
10	Excellent

In 1975 Christine Stuckelberger and her horse Granat won the highest dressage score ever awarded.

Prix—this is the level of dressage seen at the Olympic Games and World Championships. The tests at this level take eight to twelve minutes to perform.

Many FEI competitions have added a freestyle contest or kur, where you create your own routine using specified movements from the organizers. The freestyle competitions are becoming quite popular with the general public, as sometimes the programs allow you to include music that makes the horse appear to be dancing.

The tests are changed every four years to prevent horses from anticipating the exact movements, and in order to update standards.

No levels of competition allow the airs above the ground—courbette, levade, and capriole—to be included in a test or freestyle routine. The Lipizzan stallions perform these movements for demonstration purposes only

The USDF recognizes more than 700 competitions across the country. At recognized shows, you are required to braid your horse's mane so that the line of his neck is clearly visible to the judges. You are also required to use an appropriate saddle for your level of competition. Snaffle bits are a must in the lower levels, but upper levels allow a double bridle with four reins controlling a thin snaffle bit and a curb bit. The USDF issues a booklet detailing the rules for recognized shows.

The number of judges at a dressage competition varies with the size of the show, the number of rings operating simultaneously, and the number of available judges. You may see one to five judges set at certain points around the outside of the arena. From these vantage points, they can easily see how well you ride your test. Your final score should be an accurate evaluation of your ride. Each movement or figure you perform is judged against a standard of perfection. If you skip a movement, you'll receive a zero, meaning, "not executed." Scores range up to 10, which means "excellent." Achieving a 10 is extremely difficult.

Some harder moves are given a coefficient of 2, thus your score is multiplied by 2 to calculate the total score for that element.

One way to learn a great deal about dressage is to scribe for a dressage judge. A scribe sits with the judge in the judge's booth and writes down on the test sheet what the judge says. You must be able to write quickly and neatly so the scorers can calculate the final score, and so the competitor can read the judge's comments later. Most beginning dressage competitors learn a great deal from the judge's comments.

Judges look for more than the basic correctness of your test. They want to see how well your horse moves in his gaits, how good his impulsion, or desire to move forward, is, and whether the horse is relaxed and obedient. You are judged based on your position, balance, effectiveness, and whether you are in harmony with your horse—the main goal of dressage.

Once you've ridden your test, your individual scores are totaled, and then divided by the number of points possible for that test. This provides a percentage score. Generally, because 10s are so hard to achieve, scores range from 63 to 70 percent. The rules state that you must earn at least 50 percent of the maximum possible score in order to receive a prize. Throughout the 20th century, no horse ever earned as high as 80 percent on an international dressage test. Achieving 75 percent is considered remarkable. At the 1975 international level Grand Prix in Salzburg, Austria, Switzerland's Christine Stuckelberger, on Granat, set the world record score with an astounding 79.5 percent. Stuckelberger and Granat went on to win a gold medal in the individual dressage competition at the 1976 Olympics held in Montreal, Canada.

After your dressage class is over, you may pick up your test sheet from the show office and look over the judge's scores and comments. You can keep the test sheet as a reminder of what you need to work on before the next competition. Remember that you and your horse are working to achieve a harmony, and that is only attainable through determination, persistence, and practice.

Michelle Gibson rides Peron during her freestyle routine in the individual dressage competition on August 3 at the 1996 Olympics in Atlanta. Gibson finished fifth with an overall score of 222.83.

OLYMPIC DREAMS

Dressage is intriguing, challenging, and fun. But to excel in the sport, maybe even become good enough to compete in the Olympics, takes determination, persistence, and dedication.

Michelle Gibson's journey to the 1996 Olympic bronze team medal in dressage started before she took her first steps. When just a toddler, she rode with her older sisters on the family horses. By the age of five, she had figured out how to "lead" her horse Princess, an Appendix Quarter Horse, to the doghouse, pull a length of twine from a bale of hay to use as reins, mount, and ride the horse around the farm while her mother watched with an open mouth. When Michelle was nine, her family moved to Georgia, leaving behind the family horse farm in Maryland. Young Michelle was lost. Nothing could fill the void. She wasn't ready to give up riding.

After much pleading, Michelle began riding lessons at an eventing barn, where she learned the three disciplines: dressage, cross-country, and jumping. Here she found a horse named Allspice, an Appaloosa/Thoroughbred cross who loved jumping and running. With an open mind, Michelle's interest slowly focused on dressage. She began to realize that this should be the beginning of a horse's training, regardless of what discipline the horse performed later. Unable to find an experienced dressage instructor where she lived, Michelle bought a Trakehner, a breed suited to dressage, named Chausee. Now she had the right kind of horse, but she still didn't know how to teach him.

At sixteen years of age, she met Michael Poulin, who invited her to come to Maine to work and study with him. This became her goal. Still in high school, Michelle attended year round so that she could graduate early. Then, with all of her earthly possessions, she drove truck and trailer (including Chausee) to Maine to train with this top rider and trainer. She worked long hours, six days a week, learning and gaining experience at riding and training in an advanced equestrian environment.

Still in search of more knowledge, she accepted an opportunity to go to Germany for a year. Her first job was in a jumper barn. She met the German Dressage Team trainer Willi Schultheis, who hired her to teach his wife's racehorses dressage.

When her year was up, she was not ready to go home. She accepted a working student position with Rudolf Zeilinger, Willi Schultheis' master rider, and remained for two more years. She rode 8 to 12 horses a day, and learned

Michelle Gibson, shown on Peron at the 1996 Olympics, still holds the highest dressage score of any U.S. Olympic competitor.

a method of riding that worked for her and the horse. She learned a proper seat on the horse, and the importance of a horse's bloodlines. Every day was exhausting but satisfying.

Michelle had decided at sixteen that she wanted to ride on the United States Equestrian Team in the Olympics. She used to discuss her dreams with her dad when he took her to and from the barn. Realizing it would take a long time to

Overcoming All Obstacles

Not all obstacles in equestrian sports can be jumped. One young woman, Lis Hartel, was an up-and-coming dressage competitor from Denmark. She had started riding as a young girl and was winning championships in Denmark in her early twenties. Lis married, and was pregnant with her second child when, in 1944, she awoke with a stiff neck one fall day. Being an athletic woman, she shrugged it off and went about her day. But by the end of the week, her body had become paralyzed from polio.

Months passed as she lay in the hospital, praying her baby would live. Her future as an equestrian appeared over. After her baby was born healthy, Lis began to contemplate riding. Her doctors told her she might walk with canes, but she'd never ride again. She was determined to prove them wrong. Within eight months of being stricken with polio, she managed to take her first steps with canes. Her legs remained paralyzed from the knees down, but eventually, with help, she mounted her horse, Jubilee. After several falls, she learned how to balance her weight in the saddle and use tiny shifts in her weight to tell Jubilee what she wanted the horse to do.

In 1947 Lis competed again in Denmark. By 1952 she had earned the right to be one of the first women equestrians to ride in the Olympics. Lis enthralled the audience with her nearly flawless performance, despite having to be lowered onto the horse at the beginning of the ride. When she won a silver medal, tears were in many of the spectators' eyes as the individual gold medalist Henri Saint Cyr of Sweden assisted Lis up onto the podium to receive her medal.

Lis Hartel inspired riders and polio victims in countries around the world through her perseverance and dedication to her dreams and goals.

accomplish her goal, Michelle once commented, "by the time I get to the Olympics, they will be in Atlanta."

Competing in the Olympics was more than a dream to Michelle; it was her main goal in life. It was time to find a partner. She returned to the United States and started her search. The *Atlanta Journal Constitution* interviewed Michelle, and an important article followed. A woman who owned a Trakehner stallion read the article and called her. She offered to let Michelle work with the horse, Peron. He was out of shape and Michelle had to ride him in an open field, but she had a feeling it could work. She agreed to pay for all of his training, transportation, and board to get him to the Olympics.

Michelle's friends held fund-raisers on their farms to pay for Peron's airline ticket to Germany, where the horse and rider went to study with Rudolf Zeilinger for three years. They were such a beautiful pair that they became Germany's sweethearts. Their scores in the show rings increased.

At last they were ready to make their bid for the Olympic team. They had to perform in four Olympic qualifiers, which they completed with the highest scores of any American team. Back home, family and friends raised funds with newsletters and demonstrations to pay Michelle and Peron's fare to Gladstone, New Jersey, home of the United States Equestrian Team, where they earned the first seat on the team in the final qualifier. From there, they traveled to Georgia to the U.S. Olympic training center.

As a hometown girl from Roswell, Georgia, with an excellent chance to win an individual medal, Michelle was the center of local media attention at the Atlanta Olympics. Although she finished fifth, her scores were high enough to enable the American Dressage Team to win a bronze medal. Her three rides: the Grand Prix with a score of 75.20, the

Silver medallist Lis Hartel of Denmark rides her horse Jubilee, left, alongside dressage gold medallist Henri de St. Cyr of Sweden, center, and Germany's Liselott Lindsenhoff at the 1956 Olympics in Stockholm.

Grand Prix Special with a score of 74.28, and the Grand Prix Musical Freestyle with a score of 73.35, gave her a total cumulative score of 222.83. Michelle Gibson still holds the highest dressage scores in the United States.

Michelle currently teaches dressage and trains horses. She still works long days, often teaching 16 students a day. She found another high quality horse, bred in Germany, and set out to raise the money to buy him. Her next goal was to win an individual medal at the Olympics in Greece in 2004.

Dressage competition is fun and challenging at any level. But you don't have to compete to benefit from the improved communication between horse and rider, and the harmony that develops as a result of dressage training.

c. 400 B.C.	Xenophon, the Greek historian and general, creates the art of dressage
1580	Archduke Karl of Austria creates a royal stud farm in Lipizza
1600s	Royal courts across Europe develop dressage techniques
1732	The Trakehner breed is started by William I of Prussia
1735	A Hanoverian breed registry is founded at Celle, Germany
1781	Lipizzan horses are evacuated from Lipizza
1912	The United States competes in the first-ever Olympic dressage competitions at the Stockholm Olympics; Sweden wins the gold, silver, and bronze individual medals at the Stockholm Olympics
1928	Germany wins the gold medal at the first Olympic team dressage competition at the Amsterdam Olympics
1932	Piaffe and passage movements are added to Olympic dressage tests; the United States wins the bronze medal in team dressage at the Los Angeles Olympics
1936	Canter pirouettes are required for the first time at the Berlin Olympics
1945	U.S. General George Patton rescues the Lipizzans
1952	Lis Hartel of Denmark overcomes polio to win a silver medal at the Helsinki Olympics
1975	Christine Stuckelberger and Granat set a record dressage score
1976	Colonel Bengt Ljungquist writes the *Practical Dressage Manual*
1992	The United States wins the bronze medal in team dressage at the Barcelona Olympics
1996	The United States wins the bronze medal in team dressage at the Atlanta Olympics; the musical freestyle, or kur, is added to Olympic dressage competition
2000	The United States wins the bronze medal in team dressage at the Sydney Olympics

Actions—pressures applied to the horse's mouth by various bits

Capriole—a difficult leap with a kick performed by a Lipizzaner

Collected—term used to describe a horse that is well balanced under the rider

Conditioning—work that is done to keep a horse supple and fit

Counter-canter—cantering on the "wrong" lead, i.e., the outside lead when on a circle

Courbette—a complicated move in which a Lipizzaner horse, balancing on his hind legs with his forelegs off the ground, jumps

Green horse—an untrained or inexperienced horse

Hand—the unit in which a horse's height is measured; one hand equals four inches

Half-pass—moving both forward and sideways while trotting or cantering

Haute école—term used to describe the highest level of dressage

Impulsion—the energy and thrust of the horse

Kur—a freestyle dressage performance, often set to music

Lash—a short length of leather looped or left hanging on a whip or crop

Leg-yield—when a horse moves forward and diagonally away from your leg

Levade—a maneuver in which a Lipizzaner balances on its haunches at a 45-degree angle to the ground

Lunge line—a long, flat lead line that attaches to the horse's bridle, and is used to train a horse on a 20-meter circle, with or without a rider

Natural gaits—gaits that a horse is capable of performing without additional training

Overtrack—when the hind hooves step over the hoof prints of the front hooves

Passage—a slow motion trot in which the horse moves forward with a degree of suspension in each stride

Piaffe—a calm elevated trot that is performed in place

Pirouette—to turn rhythmically while remaining in one place

Round—term used to describe a horse when its neck is arched and its back muscles are rounded

Serpentine—a snaking line that touches specific points in a dressage arena

Suppling—the ability of the horse to transition smoothly and turn easily on command

Benson, Gary and Phil Maggitti. *In the Irons: Show Jumping, Dressage, and Eventing in America*. New York: Howell Book House, 1994.

Campbell, Mary. *Dancing with Your Horse*. Boonesboro, Maryland: Half Halt Press, 1989.

Crossley, Anthony. *Dressage: An Introduction*. London: Pelham Books, 1984.

Froissard, Jean. *Lipizzaners and the Spanish Riding School*. North Hollywood, California: Wilshire Book Co., 1985.

Hans-Heinrich, Isenbart, et al. *The Imperial Horse*. New York: Alfred A. Knopf, 1986.

Harris, Moira C. *Dressage by the Letter: Guide for the Novice*. New York: Howell Book House, 1997.

Henriques, Pegotty. *The Rider's Aids*. Boonsboro, Maryland: Half Halt Press, 1991.

Holderness-Roddam, Jane. *Fitness for Horse and Rider*. Devon, UK: David & Charles Publishers, 1993.

Kidd, Jane. *A Young Person's Guide to Dressage*. Warwickshire, UK: Compass Equestrian Limited, 1999.

Ljungquist, Col Bengt. *Practical Dressage Manual*. Boonsboro, Maryland: Half Halt Press, 1976.

Loriston-Clarke, Jennie. *Illustrated Guide to Dressage*. New York: Viking Penguin, 1988.

Marshall, Leonie. *Choosing a Dressage Horse*. London: J.A. Allen, 1996.

Podhajsky, Alois. *The Lipizzans*. Garden City, New York: Doubleday, 1969.

Podhajsky, Alois. *The White Stallions of Vienna*. London: Sportsman Press, 1985.

Strickland, Charlene. *Show Grooming: The Look of a Winner*. Ossining, New York: Breakthrough Publications, 1995.

Twelveponies, Mary. *Everyday Training: Backyard Dressage*. San Diego, California: AS Barnes & Co., 1980.

Von Neumann-Cosel-Nebe, Isabelle. *The Young Rider's Book of Horses & Horsemanship*, Boonesboro, Maryland: Half Halt Press, 1992.

INDEX

PICTURE CREDITS

BETTY BOLTÉ lives on a mini horse farm in Canton, Georgia, with her husband, her two children, and her father. Her daughter Danielle is training to compete in eventing. Mrs. Bolté has loved horses since she was a little girl and has attended horse shows throughout her life for the simple joy of watching horses perform. A graduate of Indiana University, Mrs. Bolté is the also the author of *Hometown Heroines*, a collection of historical biographies of 19th century American girls.